PARTY OF ONE:
A Guide to Being Single and Happy!

Foreword by
Rev. Terence E. Watts, D.Min.

Loraine Bedford

Pearly Gates Publishing LLC, Houston, Texas

PARTY OF ONE:
A Guide to Being Single and Happy!

Copyright © 2017
Loraine Bedford

All Rights Reserved.
No portion of this publication may be reproduced, stored in any electronic system, or transmitted in any form or by any means (electronic, mechanical, photocopy, recording, or otherwise) without written permission from the publisher. Brief quotations may be used in literary reviews.

Scripture references are taken from the New King James Version of the Holy Bible, unless otherwise stated. Used with permission by Zondervan.

ISBN 13: 978-1945117633
ISBN 10: 194511763X
Library of Congress Control Number: 2017935983

For information and bulk ordering, contact:
Pearly Gates Publishing LLC
Angela R. Edwards, CEO
P.O. Box 62287
Houston, TX 77205
BestSeller@PearlyGatesPublishing.com

Dedication

This book is dedicated to:

My first love, Jesus Christ. You are the reason I live, breathe, and have my being. Thank you for being patient with me and loving me in spite of my flaws and broken promises.

To every single man and woman:
You are awesome!

PARTY OF ONE

Acknowledgements

Thank you to my wonderful family: my mother, Barbara; my sisters Tee, Rita, Etta, and Velma. You guys are the best cheerleaders in the world!

To my son, Demarcus, who helped me grow up quickly: I love you!

To my friends (you know who you are) who pushed me to start and finish this project: Thank you!

To my publisher, Angela: You are awesome! Thank you for believing in me.

To my pastor, Pastor Marlin Harris: Thank you for your commitment to teaching the Word of God!

To my wonderful fiancé, Terence: All I can say is God sent you, I love you, and thank you!

Foreword

Being single and Christian in our secular society can be difficult and quite challenging at times. We struggle with what to do while waiting on God to bless us with a mate. Therein lies the crux of the problem: *What are we, as singles, to do while we wait on God for a mate?*

Loraine Bedford has been anointed by God to share His wisdom with singles concerning that vitally important question. *Party of One* deals with the wisdom gained from her journey to find acceptance and peace while living as a single Christian. Living as a single Christian can be frustrating, worrisome, and confusing when we do not understand how to live as one and do not fully comprehend how God desires to work in our lives to fulfill His purposes while we are single.

The foundational principle of this book is that responding to being single with frustration, worry, and confusion shows that we are ill-prepared for godly relationships, much less godly marriages. Being single the way God intends actually helps prepare us for godly relationships and godly marriages. Learning how to be single the way God intends also brings peace and contentment because life is not "put on hold" while waiting for that special someone. What we learn here is that God has a life full of purpose, joy, grace, and love in store for us as single Christians. The principles given in this book are biblically-based and communicated humbly from Ms. Bedford's own experience and faith journey.

PARTY OF ONE

When I met Ms. Bedford and as we developed a friendship, I noticed something different about her as a single Christian. She was confident, content, and enjoyed the life God had blessed her with as a single. She lived a life of meaning and purpose, knowing that God was working in her life. As she shared her story, I began to see some areas in my own life where I could have done things differently and even better as a single Christian. One thing I love about God, though, is that He gives us the grace we need to change! Ms. Bedford was quick to let me know she had not always been that confident and content person I had met and gotten to know. It took some time, faith, prayers, and tears to get to the place where God wanted her to be.

That is why God has given her the vision for *Party of One*; to help Christian singles avoid some of the pitfalls, dangers, and traps that will hinder them from finding peace and acceptance as singles. It is also to help give purpose and meaning to living life as singles. When one has reached that place, it is then that they are ready for a godly relationship that leads to a godly marriage. I know…because Ms. Bedford is now my fiancée! The principles learned and practiced in *Party of One* have greatly enhanced our relationship, and we are looking forward to God continuing to give us meaning and purpose in a great marriage.

Being single and Christian does not have to be sad, sorrowful, or one big pity-party. Remember Jeremiah 19:11. God has great things in store for you!

~ Rev. Terence E. Watts, D.Min.

LORAINE BEDFORD

Introduction

It was on a Sunday after church service. I was hungry and decided to drive to Conyers (an Atlanta suburb) to get breakfast at Cracker Barrel Restaurant. The restaurant is typically very busy on Sunday mornings. That morning was no different. I had to wait at least 30 minutes before being seated. While waiting, I decided to look around in the restaurant's gift shop. As I was browsing, I heard something that caught my attention, and for the next 30 minutes, I carefully observed what was actually going on around me.

"*Thompson! Party of five*", the hostess shouted over the microphone. A family of five stepped up to the podium and was escorted to their table. A few minutes later, "*Flowers! Party of seven.*" Up stepped a party of seven. I especially observed the father, mother, grandmother, three teenagers, and what looked like an eight-year-old. My eyes followed them until they were well out of my sight. **"*Hmm...interesting*"**, I thought to myself. Ten minutes later, "*Williams! Party of two.*" This time, an elderly couple stepped to the podium and was escorted to their table. I knew my name was after the Williams couple, so I eased closer to the podium because I had a plan.

About two minutes later, a manager whispered something to the hostess. She looked down at her list and spoke into the microphone again. "*Loraine! Party of...*" Before she could finish her sentence, I cut her off. **"I'm right here!"** She smiled and asked me to follow the manager to my table. I smiled, thanked her, and walked off.

I looked around at the patrons who were already seated. *Would anyone notice I was a "Party of One"? Would anyone wonder why I was having breakfast alone? Would they feel sorry for me? More importantly, was that my destiny?*

PARTY OF ONE

I was escorted to a table that was set up with two place settings. After the waiter removed the extra setting, he took my drink order and left to retrieve my water and coffee. I was left alone with my thoughts.

I stared at the fireplace and began to meditate. I asked myself the million-dollar question that I'd asked myself (and God) so many times in the past, but was never satisfied with the answer: **Why am I not married?** That time, the question prompted me to get real and 'examine myself'. I took out a piece of paper, grabbed a pen, and began to write an assessment of my life. What I discovered was this: I had been blessed to live a life of a good balance between success and failure. I listed the things I needed to change and those things I figured I was likely doing right already. At that moment, I could not foresee that three weeks later, that list would be a moot point because not only would I receive my answer, but also the peace I needed to go along with that answer.

My "single journey" - which began with a state of confusion, which led to anxiety and sometimes anger, and then acceptance and peace - has not been easy. Still, it was a journey I now realize had to be taken.

During the journey, there were times when God sent friends to walk with me and keep me encouraged. Then, there were times when I felt very alone. Looking back, I realize God was on the journey with me every day, every hour, every minute, and every second. Because He was there (and I know He will always be with me), I could finally move my life from 'neutral' to 'forward'. It all began with…

LORAINE BEDFORD

"Not that I speak in regard to need, for I have learned in whatever state I am, to be content."
(Philippians 4:11)

TABLE OF CONTENTS

DEDICATION VI

ACKNOWLEDGEMENTS VII

FOREWORD VIII

INTRODUCTION X

CHAPTER 1 - THE PROMISE 1

CHAPTER 2 - DESIRE VERSUS DESPERATION 8

CHAPTER 3 - ALONE VERSUS LONELINESS 19

CHAPTER 4 - SINGLE AND HAPPY? YES! 30

CHAPTER 5 - I'M GONNA MAKE YOU LOVE ME...NOT! WORDS OF WISDOM FOR SINGLE WOMEN 39

CHAPTER 6 - YOU WERE BORN TO LEAD...WORDS OF WISDOM FOR SINGLE MEN 50

CHAPTER 7 - SUBMISSION AND THE SINGLE CHRISTIAN 62

CHAPTER 8 - BUT GOD, SEX IS GOOD! SEX AND THE SINGLE CHRISTIAN 72

CHAPTER 9 - BEING SINGLE IS NOT A CURSE 88

CHAPTER 10 - GRACED TO BE SINGLE...WHAT IF I NEVER GET MARRIED? 104

CHAPTER 11 - WHAT TO DO WHILE YOU WAIT 112

CONCLUSION 121

ABOUT THE AUTHOR 122

Chapter 1

The Promise

"One Word from God can change your entire life." ~ Me

The year was 1983. I was 22 years old. I was visiting family in Alexandria, Louisiana when I received a prophetic Word that God was going to bless me with a husband.

I must admit, though: Before I received that Word, marriage was not on my mind, although I think it was likely in my heart.

Strange things happen to me when I receive a Word from God. I tend to grab a hold of it and meditate on it day and night. Even if it was never an issue in my life before, it becomes a major issue for me after I receive "that" Word. Deep in my heart, I have always wanted to please God. Most of my life, though, I have fallen short. So, what was at first a non-issue for me (marriage), became the central focus of my life.

About two years after receiving that Word, I moved from my hometown of Shreveport, Louisiana to Atlanta, Georgia. I had a string of disappointments in Shreveport, from relationship problems to a lack of job opportunities. I needed a change. Atlanta provided that change for me. Ups and downs awaited me, but I did fall in love with the city…and my quest to find a suitable husband began. Thus, my first mistake.

"He who finds a wife finds a good thing and obtains favor from the LORD."
(Proverbs 18:22)

THE PROMISE

Proverbs 18:22 makes it very clear that God did not create me to seek a husband, but for my husband to seek me. I, as a Christian adult, have always been a regular church-goer. I'd heard that passage of Scripture read from the pulpit many times. I knew the Scripture from memory AND it had been quoted to me many times by people who were constantly encouraging me to patiently wait for a mate. Some would say, *"Just wait; he'll find you"*. Others would tell me, *"You don't have to look for a husband. He'll come just when you stop looking"*. Still more would say, *"You're too consumed with the idea of finding a husband. Focus on something else and God will send your husband"*.

Can I be honest with you?

Every time someone would offer me those bits of advice or nuggets of wisdom, I wanted to **SCREAM**!

Usually, the person offering the advice was already married - which made it even worse! However, I listened to their advice. Over and over, I tried my best to focus on other things. Even when I convinced myself that I would just "relax, relate, release" and allow God to bless me with a husband, trust me: My desire for a mate was always at the forefront of my thinking.

Hindsight is always 20/20. Had I known then what I know now, I would have handled things differently. I want to share the things I have learned over the many years of being single and desiring marriage. Allow me to share with you how I went from being *desperate* for a mate to *desiring* a mate.

PARTY OF ONE

Questions to Ponder from Chapter 1

1. Has God made you a promise that has not manifested in your life? What is that specific promise and how long ago did He make that promise to you?

THE PROMISE

2. Have you ever been tempted to doubt you actually heard from God? How do you keep yourself encouraged until your promise is manifested?

PARTY OF ONE

3. Have you recognized any "triggers" that make you feel like you want to give up, cave in, and quit waiting on God? What are those triggers?

___

___

___

___

___

___

___

___

___

___

___

___

___

___

___

___

___

___

THE PROMISE

4. Had you known "then" what you know now, how would you approach dating and singleness?

5. What advice have you been given that helps you to not get discouraged about your singleness?

CHAPTER 2

Desire versus Desperation

Desire:
To long or hope for.

Desperation:
Suffering extreme need or anxiety; involving or employing extreme measures in an attempt to escape defeat or frustration.

"Desperate people do desperate things."

What most people call 'desire' is actually 'desperation'. I believe desire and desperation come from the same place: the soul. Man is a three-part being.

Man is a *spirit*.

Man possess a *soul*.

Man lives in a *body*.

It's the soul realm that we - as people - struggle the most with. After all, the soul is where our emotions are. It's where we feel and these feelings guide our choices. The soul is where some of our desires come from. While not all of our desires come from God, certainly a lot of desires do.

PARTY OF ONE

There is absolutely nothing wrong with desiring to be married. It's a desire that was imparted in us by God. After all, God made woman for man and man for woman. It was God who created Eve so Adam wouldn't be alone. When Adam looked around the animal kingdom he had responsibility for caring over, he found no suitable mate for himself. So, God put him to sleep and created a woman from the man.

It's no wonder we desire each other. Imagine being a man, waking up, and seeing that God has created a beautiful creation that looks almost identical to you! She has two arms and two legs. Unlike most of the animal kingdom, she walks upright. She has beautiful hair and eyes. Then, the man looks closer and notices a few differences. Hmm... She has hips. She's softer to the touch. She walks with a twist. She has breasts. *(Remember: God created a WOMAN, not a baby girl.)* Her sexual organs are different. Interesting! Adam had to have been beside himself! This being God created was beautiful! Adam was pleased and was immediately drawn to her.

"The man said, "This is now bone of my bones, and flesh of my flesh; she shall be called Woman, because she was taken out of Man."
(Genesis 2:23, NASB)

That 'drawing' - the attraction - came from God. God purposely created Eve so that Adam would be drawn to her. Adam immediately recognized Eve was created just for him. He immediately had a desire for her.

Nothing has changed from the days of Adam and Eve. Men still desire women - and women still desire men. Thank God!

DESIRE VERSUS DESPERATION

One thing to notice about Adam was that he was not desperate. He had a desire, yes; but he was not desperate. Nowhere in the Bible will you read that Adam thought he couldn't live or be happy if God didn't create a suitable mate for him. Adam never stopped doing what he was assigned to do (tilling the Garden, taking care of the animals, walking and talking with God) just because he didn't have a mate.

Adam never said, "*I'm never going to be happy until God sends me a mate*" or "*I'm never going on my dream vacation until God sends me a wife*". Neither did he get depressed because none of the animals were suitable for him. Nope. Adam was busy naming animals, taking care of the Garden, and talking to God. He was busy doing what God told him he was supposed to do. Then, all of a sudden, here comes a woman who was suitable for him! Adam recognized the desire for a helper, but he was not desperate.

Desperation can become a god.

"*You shall not make other gods besides Me; gods of silver or gods of gold, you shall not make for yourselves.*"
(Exodus 20:23, NASB)

The difference between desire and desperation is impatience. Desperation creates the unwillingness to wait - coupled with a willingness to do anything to get what you want. Men and women can sense desperation 10 miles away. Have you ever seen a woman who dresses very provocatively, showing body parts that only her husband should see? Desperate! Have you ever seen a man wearing jeans so tight, you can't figure out how he's breathing? Desperate!

PARTY OF ONE

I can tell you story after story about men I've dated who barely knew my last name, yet they were ready and willing to marry me after the second or third date. I mean, honestly: Do you really think talking marriage to a person you've known for a mere two months will endear them to you? I remember being so turned off when the subject of marriage came up. But you know what? I was doing the same thing! I didn't talk about marriage to men after two months, **BUT** it didn't take long for me to become possessive after about four or five dates.

The desperation *(not desire)* to be married had become my god. The desperation for marriage was an idol to me, although I didn't see it that way. When impatience infiltrated my desire, it became an idol to me. I wanted marriage at all costs. It was all I thought about. Hey, I didn't have a golden calf in my house, so I didn't see my desperation to be married as an "idol"…but it was. An idol is anything - any desire or any person who becomes more important to you than your relationship with God. This includes insisting on having things my way or according to my timing or how I want it. To be perfectly honest, God was number two on my list of priorities at the time. God came only after my impatient desire to be married.

That was hard to admit then. It's still hard to admit even now…but it's the truth.

Do you want to know one of the things that kept me in that pitiful state for so long? I hate to admit this, but I can honestly say that one of my biggest mistakes was having friends who were equally desperate for marriage. We would have daily or weekly conversations about our impatient **desires**…I mean *desperations*. This possibly kept me in a state of desperation a lot longer than I would have been had I not surrounded myself with people who were as desperate as I was.

DESIRE VERSUS DESPERATION

How do you know when desperation has become a god in your life? As a former "idol-worshipper", I am glad to share some signs with you that you can use as a checklist to examine yourself:

1. You become sad or depressed at the news of an impending marriage of a loved-one or friend.
2. You will not go on that dream vacation (Paris, Hawaii, Italy, etc.) until God sends you your husband/wife. You will try to force the issue when you get tired of waiting. You need a husband/wife to justify going, without understanding the two are not necessarily connected.
3. Every man/woman you meet, you wonder if he/she could be your husband/wife.
4. You won't buy real estate until God sends you a mate. After all, you don't want to buy a house he/she might not like, so you are just going to wait. Then, you will try to rush into a relationship because not only are you tired of waiting for a mate, you now desperately want your dream house!
5. Church has become a "meat market" instead of House of Prayer.
6. Every sermon the Pastor preaches, you are listening for a "Word about your mate" instead of seeking a Word from God about how to please Him in every area of your life.
7. When people ask you, *"When are you going to get married?"*, you become defensive and sad. You rush into relationships simply to avoid having to answer that question.
8. You don't want to run into family and friends you haven't seen in years because you are afraid they are going to ask if you're married, and guess what? You're not! See number seven (frustrated!).

9. You are angry with God because you're not married. Most people will not admit to this, but the truth is that a lot of Christian men and women blame God because of their single status.
10. You don't appreciate the blessings you have because you spend too much time focusing on that one thing you don't have…a mate.

This list is not all-inclusive. There are so many other signs that you are desperate and have made desperation to be married into an idol. If you recognize any of those signs in yourself, here are a few things you can do to overcome desperation:

1. Confess to God the way you feel.
2. Repent. Repent for being jealous. Repent for being unappreciative, angry, frustrated, etc.
3. Take communion as a way of sealing your deliverance from those signs of desperation.
4. Begin to speak daily confessions over your life that will keep you encouraged and appreciative.
5. Spend quality time with people who will keep you encouraged. Iron sharpens iron!
6. Become a giver to someone less fortunate as a way of getting your mind off of yourself. Getting delivered from self is the remedy from those signs.
7. Cultivate a thankful spirit. Become appreciative for everything and everyone God has blessed you with.

DESIRE VERSUS DESPERATION

Questions to Ponder from Chapter 2

1. After reading Chapter 2, would you define your present state as (1) content and happy, yet desiring a mate, (2) desperate for a mate, or (3) content and happy as a single without a desire for a mate?

PARTY OF ONE

2. Why do you think Adam knew someone/something was missing in his life?

DESIRE VERSUS DESPERATION

3. The difference between desire and desperation is impatience. What are some of the mistakes you have made as a result of your impatience?

_____

_____

_____

_____

_____

_____

_____

_____

_____

_____

_____

_____

_____

_____

_____

PARTY OF ONE

4. Identify any person or situation in your life that might be keeping you in a state of desperation because of their desperation or negative feelings towards singleness.

_____

_____

_____

_____

_____

_____

_____

_____

_____

_____

_____

_____

_____

_____

DESIRE VERSUS DESPERATION

5. Name three (3) things you can do immediately to move from desperation to desire.

_____

_____

_____

_____

_____

_____

_____

_____

_____

_____

_____

_____

_____

_____

_____

_____

Chapter 3

Alone versus Loneliness

"God said, "It's not good for the man to be alone. I'll make him a helper, a companion.""
(Genesis 2:18, MSG)

Alone:
Separate, apart, or isolated from others.

Lonely:
Affected with, characterized by, or causing a depressing feeling of being alone.

I often hear people use the words 'lonely' and 'alone' interchangeably, even though they are two different words with two different meanings. You can be alone and not be lonely. You can also be lonely without being alone.

I once heard a married person with young children speak about how lonely she was. I can relate to both sides. I spend a lot of time alone, but I hardly ever feel lonely...anymore. However, I've also been in a crowd of people and felt very lonely.

ALONE VERSUS LONELINESS

I remember attending a party where there was music, food, and a house filled with people laughing, playing cards, dancing, eating, having conversations, etc. I can honestly tell you that I felt like I was in a dark room all alone. I attended the party because the host invited me. The problem was the host was the only person I knew at the party, and she was busy entertaining her guests. At the time, I was much too shy to approach people and introduce myself, so I just stood around like a fly on the wall while listening to others' conversations - and eating everything in sight.

That night, food became my companion - but that's another story for another book...

One of the reasons many singles get into unhealthy relationships is because we don't want to be lonely. I have never been married, but I can tell you from testimony after testimony of my family and friends who are married, widowed, or divorced: Marriage is not the cure for loneliness.

I once heard a wise Pastor say, "*If you think you feel bad because you're lonely as a single person, talk to someone who is married and lonely. That's worse!*" The advantage a single person has over a married person when it comes to loneliness is the fact that the single person has HOPE that one day, it will not be that way - while a lonely married person is wondering, "*Man! Is this the way it's going to be for the rest of my life?*"

Hopelessness sets in...

PARTY OF ONE

Genesis 2:18 states, "*And the Lord God said, "It is not good for the man to be alone. I will make a helper suitable for him."*" I remember reading that and thinking, **"If there's nothing wrong with being single, then why did God say 'it is not good that man should be alone'?"** Consider this: At the time God spoke those words, Adam was the only man on Earth. Adam was surrounded by two things: (1) The presence of God, and (2) animals. Adam had already recognized that none of the animals were a suitable helpmeet for him (see Genesis 2:20). God had a plan for mankind, and He chose to fulfill that plan with the involvement of a woman - which is why He created Eve. God wasn't saying it's not good for man to be single; He was stating it's not good for man to be alone because he needs a female partner (a wife) to fulfill His plan for the Earth and mankind!

Every bad relationship I have been involved in started because I was lonely. I wanted someone to spend time with, someone to talk to, and someone to give me that attention I was so desperately seeking. I was not comfortable spending time alone - and I definitely didn't believe my relationship with God was enough to fulfill my human needs.

Relationships built on loneliness can easily become toxic. Because of loneliness, I put up with bad behaviors which included broken promises, lies, cheating, and downright disrespect. After I finally woke up and decided I'd had enough of those behaviors, I was right back where I started: lonely.

So, I guess by now you may be wondering how I finally overcame that behavior. I'm happy to share that with you!

ALONE VERSUS LONELINESS

One Sunday evening, I was watching Christian TV. A minister was ministering to a church filled with women. He encouraged them to begin to appreciate and love themselves by not waiting for another person to treat them special. Instead, they should learn to love themselves enough to do all those special things for themselves. He suggested they get up, get dressed up, made up, and take themselves out to dinner. He suggested they take themselves to a nice movie, a nice restaurant, etc. I listened intently and decided to take to heart and put into practice everything he talked about during that 30-minute segment.

The following Saturday, I took myself to a movie. I also took the time to dress up and look good as if I were going out on a date with a man. After enjoying the movie, it was time to move on to dinner. As soon as I arrived at the restaurant and the hostess realized I was a **party of one**, she immediately invited me to sit at the bar.

"No. I would like a table, please", was my response.

A few minutes later, I was escorted to a table where for the next hour, I enjoyed my dinner. I also spent a great deal of time looking around at people who were eating with others, contemplating if they wondered why I was alone. In other words, I felt somewhat uncomfortable. However, as I continued to take myself out to restaurants, I no longer paid attention to nor cared about what others thought. I began to not only enjoy my time alone; I began to look forward to it while enjoying my meals!

PARTY OF ONE

Proverbs 18:24 teaches us that we must show ourselves friendly if we want to have friends. All of us need a community of people to engage with. We were not created to be a 'lone ranger' in this world. God created us to depend on each other. While you don't need a husband/wife in order to not be lonely, you do need relationships with others to avoid loneliness. Those relationships include family, friends, neighbors, community, church members, co-workers, etc. If you are lonely, yet you have a hard time making friends, you will have to come out of your comfort zone and do things you are uncomfortable doing.

First, stop turning down invitations to events that you are invited to. Join a meet-up group of people who share your interests. Don't just be a Sunday morning church-goer. Volunteer for a ministry at your church. This is a great opportunity to connect with others and build relationships. I met the vast majority of my friends at church while volunteering for ministry. The fact that we are a part of the same ministry means we have something in common.

If no one invites you to fellowship, then take the initiative and invite others. You can invite your ministry co-laborers to your home for a potluck dinner or for a game night. Suggest that a group of you get together and go see a movie or play. Exchange phone numbers with the group, then call and genuinely check on them and their family. Offer to pray for them if they are facing challenges. Trust me: When you begin to show people you genuinely care about them and are praying for them, you will begin to bond with them because everyone wants people who care about them!

ALONE VERSUS LONELINESS

What I'm trying to tell you is that you don't have to be lonely just because you are single. We all have been given family, friends, jobs, churches, etc. so that we can be a part of communities. Please take advantage of all the available resources to ensure you are living a full, well-rounded, balanced, and happy life.

PARTY OF ONE

Questions to Ponder from Chapter 3

1. Think back on a time when you felt lonely. Did you ever make the mistake of seeking out companionship for the sole reason of overcoming loneliness? How did that relationship work out?

_____

_____

_____

_____

_____

_____

_____

_____

_____

_____

_____

_____

ALONE VERSUS LONELINESS

2. What are some things you can personally do to overcome those lonely feelings? Are you willing to step out of your comfort zone to meet people and seek out new adventures that will put you in the presence of people who you may have never met?

_____

_____

_____

_____

_____

_____

_____

_____

_____

_____

_____

_____

_____

PARTY OF ONE

3. After reading Chapter 2 of Genesis, do you think Adam was lonely? Why or why not?

ALONE VERSUS LONELINESS

4. <u>Challenge #1:</u> If you have been uncomfortable going places alone, challenge yourself this week to do something alone so that you can get accustomed to enjoying spending time with yourself...alone. Some suggestions are: dinner, movie, a play, visit a museum, attend a concert, etc. Below, write about your experience. How did it feel? Will you do it again? What's your next adventure alone?

_____

_____

_____

_____

_____

_____

_____

_____

_____

_____

_____

_____

5. <u>Challenge #2:</u> Think of something fun you have never done before that you are willing to give a try. Now, search the internet for a group of people with the same interest and make plans to at least attend a meeting. For example, if you've never been skiing because no one in your inner-circle skis, search for a group that takes annual ski trips. Attend one of their meetings for the sole purpose of information-gathering. Think seriously about joining them on their next trip. Write about the experience. Where did you go? Why did you choose that specific activity? What adventure would you like to go on next?

Chapter 4

Single and Happy? Yes!

Too many single people think the words 'single' and 'happy' can't be used in the same sentence. I'm here to tell you they can. I'm not talking about the "fake" happiness that so many men and women try to convince themselves and their friends they have. I'm talking about a **JOY** that you have, no matter what your circumstances are.

Possessing true happiness during your single years depends so much on how you view being single. If most of your friends are married and you're ashamed that you're single, you will not experience joy while being single. If you are sitting back waiting to see who is next in line to divorce so you can feel better about being single, you're not happy. If your happiness depends on someone else's downfall, not only are you not happy, you are truly a sad person who is harboring and nourishing a vindictive spirit.

I remember when I was unhappily single. When married people would ask me, *"When are you getting married?"*, I would always answer with, **"I don't know"**. But let me tell you what I was really thinking.

(I rehearsed the following brief conversation in my mind many times and was waiting for the right opportunity to use it.)

PARTY OF ONE

Married Person: "*When are you getting married? I can't believe you haven't met the right man yet and had a house filled with babies!*"

Me: "*No, I haven't met the right man yet, so I have no idea when I'm getting married. However, I was reading an article online the other day, and it stated that greater than 50% of all marriages in America end in divorce. So, wouldn't it be better if I asked you, "When are you getting a divorce - since your chances of getting one are a lot higher than my chances of getting married?"*"

Drop the mic.

Walk away.

Now, I must admit: I never had that conversation with anyone, and I am so glad I didn't. You know what that represents? It represents a person who is very bitter and sad about being single. It represents a person who is ashamed of being single and angry at people for assuming something must be wrong with me because I'm single. It also represents a person who is ungrateful for all the great things about his or her life. A person who spends so much time focused on what they don't have, rarely stops to appreciate what they do have.

Because marriage was such a powerful desire in my life, I had to learn to be happy while single. I started by expressing my appreciation for all the great people and things in my life. I started praising God, even when I didn't feel like praising Him. I taped post-it notes with positive affirmations written on them to my bathroom mirror to remind myself to confess how blessed I was every day.

SINGLE AND HAPPY? YES!

There were days when I would get up and get ready for work or church and not want to say those confessions. I knew that would happen, so I taped them to the dashboard of my car as well. At some point during the day, I had to speak those confessions. I had to remind myself that God is bigger than any situation in my life. I actually had to remind myself each day that God loves me and wants what's best for me. He would never withhold any good thing from me!

Next, I had to work on not comparing myself or my life to other people or their lives. Asking God why so-and-so was getting married for the second, third, or fourth time and I hadn't been blessed with a husband didn't help my situation. I eventually learned that what God does in another person's life has nothing to do with me - and it's not my business. Once I accepted that and learned to rejoice with those who rejoice, I knew I was one step closer to being a **HAPPY** single person.

I then had to make sure I was not spending too much time with people who were as desperate as what I was trying to overcome. I started backing away from friendships with people whose conversations were all about, **"When, God? When?"** I lost some friendships during that season of my life, but I have no regrets. I still love those people, but it was necessary to cut ties in order to move on to the next season of my life. Some of the friendships ended because of misunderstandings, and one or two others because I (or they) decided to back away. Either way, I am confident God orchestrated the breaks. I am in a better place because of it - and I'm certain they are, too. Do I miss them? At first, I missed them every day. Some I cried over. Others I didn't. You know what? In due season, God added to my life the type of people I needed to get through the next season.

PARTY OF ONE

After all of that, I was still not quite sure where God wanted me to be. I thank God for ministers. God allowed me to hear a sermon that changed my life. The sermon was preached by a pastor's wife and when I heard it, I was floored. When I say 'floored', I don't mean in a shouting, running-around-the-church kind of way. I was floored in the sense that I had to drop to my knees and repent. The message didn't so much inspire me as it did convict me.

The Woman of God talked about how so many of us are in love with God, but we need to admit we are angry with Him because He has not manifested different promises in our lives. Hours after hearing that sermon, I could not get it off my mind, so I sent her a private message - and she responded! Thank God! She inspired me and suggested some things for me to read (which I did). From that moment forward, I was a changed person. The feelings of desperation left me completely, and I had a peace that I could not explain.

The process I just described didn't happen overnight. It took years. Because of my experience, it doesn't have to take you years to learn what I learned. The reason I had to walk that path was so I could write this book and save you from some of the frustrations I experienced. You can take what I had to learn the 'hard way' and use it in your life so that you don't repeat my mistakes.

One thing I'm sure of is this:

I'm a living witness! You **CAN** be single and happy!

SINGLE AND HAPPY? YES!

Questions to Ponder from Chapter 4

1. Do you struggle with a response when people ask you why you're not married yet? Do you become embarrassed or defensive? Why or why not?

_____

_____

_____

_____

_____

_____

_____

_____

_____

_____

_____

_____

_____

_____

2. After reading this chapter, what do you think is an appropriate response to the 'why aren't you married yet' question?

SINGLE AND HAPPY? YES!

3. If you are an unhappy unmarried person, why do you think you are so unhappy? Meditate on some things you can do to overcome your unhappiness. Write those ideas below.

PARTY OF ONE

4. Have you ever felt as if God was withholding a mate from you because of some past sin? If so, has it affected your relationship with God?

SINGLE AND HAPPY? YES!

5. Examine your friendships. Are there people in your life who are hindering you from growing in this area? If so, what are you going to do about it?

_____

_____

_____

_____

_____

_____

_____

_____

_____

_____

_____

_____

_____

_____

_____

Chapter 5

I'm Gonna Make You Love Me...NOT!
Words of Wisdom for Single Women

"I praise You because I am fearfully and wonderfully made; your works are wonderful, I know that full well."
(Psalm 139:14, NIV)

I am amazed at the number of men and women I know who think they can do things that will **make** someone love them. Some men are guilty of using money and power to try to get the love they are desperate for. Some women often use their bodies (and even children) to try to force a man to love them. Money, power, a nice body, and children are all wonderful things to possess - as long as they do not possess you. You must understand this: Those things will only draw people to you. They may even get them to marry you. **BUT** they will never make them love you. True love runs so deep, it can never be purchased with power and money.

Remember: The greatest and most perfect love of all is the love God has for you. He loves you so much, He sent His Son to Earth to die a horrible death for your sins so that you can be reconciled to Him. Jesus literally paid the penalty for our salvation. He didn't do it with money. He did so with His blood. This penalty consisted of His life and His blood for your salvation, peace, freedom, health, and so much more. This love means someone is willing to die for you. This also means true love can only be given; it can never be bought nor sold - particularly as it relates to relationships between men and women.

I'M GONNA MAKE YOU LOVE ME...NOT!

Earlier, I mentioned women who will use their precious children to try to manipulate a man into loving them. Every time I hear about it or witness that type of behavior, I am reminded of one of the most interesting accounts in the Bible *(which can be found in the Book of Genesis)*. The story of one man, Jacob, and two sisters, Leah and Rachel, is one that really hits home - even today. Jacob, the son of Isaac and grandson of Abraham, was known as a 'trickster'. In order to get a good understanding of the type of man Jacob was, please take some time now to read Genesis Chapters 27-33.

Don't worry. It's okay. I'll wait...

Great! You're back!

One of the first things to notice is after Jacob met Rachel, he fell madly in love with her. The Bible makes it clear that Rachel was a very beautiful woman. However, there had to be other qualities besides her beautiful face and fine shape Jacob noticed in her that kept his attention. How do I know that? Well, for starters, when Laban (Rachel's father) offered to pay Jacob wages for working for him, the only thing Jacob wanted was to marry Rachel. Had Rachel been beautiful but mean or disrespectful, I doubt he would have found her as irresistible as he did.

Jacob offered to work seven long years for the opportunity to marry Rachel. Now, I've met some persistent men in my day, but none like Jacob. That man worked every day for seven years to get the woman he wanted, and the Bible states those seven years seemed like only a few days to him because of his love for Rachel. Some men are not willing to work that hard and that long for the opportunity to marry a woman, especially when they can't so much as hold her hand until they marry!

PARTY OF ONE

The story continues...

After seven years had passed, Jacob went to Laban and asked for his wife. Laban tricked Jacob into marrying his older daughter, Leah, first. Guess what Jacob did? He ended up working an additional seven years for Rachel's hand. That's **FOURTEEN YEARS** of working to pay off the debt to a father who didn't have enough integrity to honor his original promise.

When a man finds a woman he desires, he will do extraordinary things. He has a willingness to do whatever he has to do to show her he desires her. There is nothing she has to do (outside of showing a little interest) to get his attention. The opposite is true when a man doesn't want a certain woman. There is nothing she can do to make him love her.

Jacob **LOVED** Rachel, but he *TOLERATED* Leah.

I've known women who purposely got pregnant in order to get the man to love them and (eventually) marry them. Listen ladies: If he doesn't already love you before you get pregnant, getting pregnant will not make him love you afterwards. He might get temporarily excited about the thought of having a child, but don't mistake his excitement for love.

Jacob's relationship with Leah is a perfect example of that. You have to understand how important it was for a woman to give her husband children during the Old Testament days. When a woman was unable to bear children for her husband, it brought a sense of shame to her. Although Rachel was very much loved by her husband, she was barren. During Rachel's time of experiencing the pain of being barren, Leah became pregnant and gave birth to Jacob's first son, Reuben.

I'M GONNA MAKE YOU LOVE ME...NOT!

After giving birth to Reuben, Leah said, "*It is because the Lord has seen my misery. Surely, my husband will love me now.*" But Jacob **still** didn't express any love towards Leah. She became pregnant a second time and gave birth to her second son, Simeon. After the birth of Simeon, Leah said, "*Because the Lord heard that I am not loved, he gave me this one, too.*" **Still**, Jacob did not express any love towards Leah. His heart was still solely with Rachel, though she was barren. Leah became pregnant with her third son, Levi, with the hopes that Jacob will love her. She said, "*Now my husband will become attached to me because I have borne him three sons.*" In all three instances, the focus was solely on trying to get Jacob to love her. In all three instances, she was met with disappointment.

Do you see a pattern here? Each time Leah became pregnant, she hoped that each child would draw Jacob closer to her and make him love her. It never happened. As a matter of fact, Leah had seven children with Jacob (six sons and one daughter), and not a single one of those births turned Jacob's heart towards her. She bore him seven children, yet he never fell in love with, nor desired her.

How many children have you brought into this world, hoping with each one that you would receive the love you are so desperate for? Just like Leah, you are taking desperate measures to make someone love you. It will not work. It did not work for Leah, and it will not work for you. Even if you get pregnant, get married, and have the baby, won't you always wonder if he really married you because he loves you **or** because he felt it was the 'right thing to do'?

PARTY OF ONE

Laban convinced Jacob to marry Leah first by telling him it was the "right thing to do". Yet, Leah never experienced the love of someone who actually wanted her just for who she was. In my opinion, the only thing Laban did was set his oldest daughter up for a lifetime of marriage to a man who didn't want her and whose heart was always with her sister, Rachel.

God desires so much more for you than that. He doesn't want you to be someone's "Plan B" (Leah). He wants you to be the woman your man had to work long and hard to get (Rachel) because he desires you. You are the one he is willing to work 14 long years for to become his wife. You are the one worth every romantic dinner, every dozen roses, and every piece of jewelry. Men work hard for their resources, and you are worth every penny. Real men love to work and hunt. Do you hear me? **THEY LOVE IT!** As a matter of fact, they have a habit of not being appreciative of anything nor anyone they didn't have to work hard to get. Do not take that God-given gift from them by reversing the roles. Their role is to hunt. Yours is to wait on and serve the Lord. Don't fear missing your opportunity to meet the right person. Just **BE** the right person God wants you to be, and your man will spot you from miles away. This is God's promise: If you focus on developing the qualities God wants you to have, you will not miss out on the man God has for you. Take God at His Word and trust what He says. **HE IS THE MATCHMAKER!**

Oh yeah, by the way: Rachel eventually bore two sons for her husband.

I would rather be single my entire life than experience the type of marriage Leah had to endure. However, if you truly desire a mate, you can begin your preparation right now to receive your mate. How? Well, I'll tell you!

I'M GONNA MAKE YOU LOVE ME...NOT!

First, learn how to take care of a household. You know...those pesky things that likely drive you nuts in the moment:

- Budgeting
- Cooking
- Cleaning
- Submitting

Submission? Yep! Submission. How did 'submission' make the list? That topic will be discussed in depth later...

One last word to the women: If you don't remember anything else, please remember this:

A MAN WILL NOT FILL THAT EMPTY HOLE IN YOUR SOUL.

If you feel incomplete and lonely, you are wrong to think it's because you need a man. That emptiness in you is where a special relationship with God belongs, and no one else can fill that void - regardless of how much they love you or how hard they try to please you. No person is your all-in-all. Many women have gone through numerous men because they are looking for that special person who will close that huge hole in their soul. It never happens. Put God first. Develop an intimate and personal love relationship with Him, and you'll see how much better your other relationships will develop.

That's **GOD'S** promise!

PARTY OF ONE

Questions (for Ladies) to Ponder from Chapter 5

1. Have you ever been so desperate for a relationship that you dated someone without him having to do anything to pursue you? In the end, how did that make you feel? What will you do differently next time?

I'M GONNA MAKE YOU LOVE ME...NOT!

2. Think about Leah. How do you think she felt day in and day out, being with a man who she knew didn't love her? Have you ever been in a relationship where you felt tolerated instead of loved? How did you free yourself from that relationship?

PARTY OF ONE

3. Now, think about Rachel. Rachel felt terrible because she was unable to bear children. Is there an area in your life you feel is lacking and you are ashamed? Has not having a husband made you feel ashamed? How do you deal with that (or any lack in your life) on a daily basis? What can you do to overcome your feelings of shame?

_____

_____

_____

_____

_____

_____

_____

_____

_____

_____

_____

_____

_____

I'M GONNA MAKE YOU LOVE ME...NOT!

4. How far have you gone to get someone to love you? How do you feel today about the extreme measures you took to try to get the love you desperately wanted?

_____
_____
_____
_____
_____
_____
_____
_____
_____
_____
_____
_____
_____
_____
_____

PARTY OF ONE

5. Each time Leah became pregnant, she hoped Jacob would fall in love with her. What advice would you give the 'Leahs' in your life who keep doing extreme things and getting no positive results?

Chapter 6

You Were Born to Lead
Words of Wisdom for Single Men

On the sixth day, when God was creating the Earth, He created living creatures that moved along the ground, and wild animals, each according to its kind. Then, God created man. Do you know in whose likeness God created man? **HIMSELF**! God created man in His own image! God took everything wonderful about Himself (which is everything), and breathed **HIMSELF** into man. A part of being in God's image is you have His Spirit. In other words, you are just like your Father!

One day, while sitting in the library, I began to read the Book of Genesis. I noticed something I had never noticed in all the years of reading the Bible: Genesis 2:4-6 tells us that when God first made the Earth and the Heavens, the Earth did not have any shrubs or plants because God had not sent rain on the Earth. Why is that significant? Because there was no man to cultivate the ground! The job of tilling the grounds was left to man - not because God couldn't do it Himself, but because God created man for a purpose. Man's main purpose on this Earth is to worship God, serve God, and have dominion over the Earth. That includes managing the Earth and taking care of it. Toiling (hard and continuous work) for man came **after** the fall of mankind (see Genesis 3:17-19). Until then, everything was provided for him by God. All man had to do was take care of it, which was a pleasure for him because it gave him purpose and meaning in his life.

PARTY OF ONE

A real man must have purpose and meaning. The first thing man had that was already prepared for him when he came to Earth was a vocation…a calling. Genesis also teaches us that God planted a garden in the East (in Eden), and that's where He put man after He created him. So, the second thing man had already prepared for him was a place to live.

God also made all kinds of trees that were good for food. So, the third thing man had already prepared for him was food and water. Notice there was a river flowing through Eden. Looks to me like God prepared for man's arrival on Earth by providing everything he needed to live a successful life!

Let's review this: Man had purpose and meaning, a place to live, food, and water. What came *after* all of that preparation? A wife.

What that taught me is this: A man needs to have accomplished a certain level of independence before he considers taking on the responsibility of a wife. Questions: If you are a man who has the desire to be married, have you properly prepared yourself to receive a wife? Do you have a job or some type of income? Do you have a place of your own to live? Can you provide the basic necessities it takes to live on your own before inviting a woman into your space to share your life? You see, when Eve showed up, everything was already prepared for her. She lacked **nothing**.

YOU WERE BORN TO LEAD

One thing God did after He created the woman (and I absolutely *LOVE* this) was **HE** (God) presented her to the man! God Himself introduced Adam to his bride, Eve. Now **THAT** was a match made in Heaven...literally! Needless to say, Adam was very pleased and liked what he saw. God knew exactly what Adam desired and needed (just as he knows what you desire and need), and He created a woman that pleased the man. Eve didn't arrive one minute late nor one minute early.

If you are a single man who truly desires to be married, remember this: As a man, it is important to prepare for a wife. However, preparing does not have to be a depressing thing. Your preparation time can include doing things like completing your education, working a job, budgeting your household income, learning to be a maintenance man, a yard man, a father, money manager, and yes, even a cook. The most important thing, though, to do during your preparation time is to train yourself to hear the voice of God. Hearing from God is a must if you are to be the leader God wants you to be in your family. Your family will depend on you to have sound judgment and make good decisions that will affect not only you, but your wife and children. I obviously cannot tell you what it means to be a man, but I can certainly tell you that if you haven't prepared to be responsible without a woman around, you are not prepared to be responsible with a family.

PARTY OF ONE

Emotional Baggage

Another way to prepare is to work on getting rid of any emotional baggage you bring with you from your childhood or past relationships. If you are wounded in any way, seek healing. Talk to a counselor or seek out a mentor who can pray with you and help you overcome your emotional wounds. No woman wants to live with a man who is hellbent on making her pay for his past hurts, whether he's doing it consciously or unconsciously.

Jealousy

If you possess a jealous spirit, ask God to deliver you from it. Jealousy comes from a place of insecurity. I've known men who get angry because their wife or girlfriend held innocent conversations with other men. I'm not talking about strange men. I'm referring to men they may run into that they used to attend school with or whom they grew up with in the same neighborhood or church.

Consider this: Your woman had a life before she met you. That life consisted of a lot of people and relationships at different levels. It is very rude to not acknowledge someone you know simply because you're out with your significant other. She should always be respectful to the man in her life. She should introduce acquaintances to her beau and not do or say anything that can be interpreted as disrespectful. Her relationships and friendships are important to her, and she should be confident they can be balanced. If you are dating a woman and the two of you run into someone she knows, trust her and give her the benefit of the doubt. Even if the person is an ex-boyfriend or ex-husband, she deserves your trust.

YOU WERE BORN TO LEAD

Possessing a jealous spirit can kill a relationship quicker than almost anything. A woman will not feel free to be herself around you if you are the jealous type. If she cannot be herself around you for fear you might start to feel insecure, you will never get to know the true 'her'. Now, if you have a woman who continually does things to disrespect you, then, at the very least, you know what kind of woman you're dealing with. That knowledge will allow you to make an informed decision about the direction of the relationship based upon what you know - not on what you imagine.

Finances

I often hear men make the statement that all women want is a man with money. That's a very broad statement - one that is not true for the vast majority of women. However, we all know that finances are important. We live in a society where the law of exchange prevails. If you go to the grocery store right now, you can get all the fruits, vegetables, rice, and bread they have available; however, before you walk out of the store, you must make an exchange. They will exchange that food for your money. They don't care if you are male or female, rich or poor, saved or sinner. You must pay for your groceries before you walk out the door!

Certainly, money is **not** the most important thing in a marriage, but it is one of the important things that aid in the success of a marriage. If your finances are a mess, you are not ready to get married. You must be able to manage your finances before you get married. If your finances are out of control, seek advice from a wise money manager. Trust me: The work you put in now will save you a lot of grief once you have a family.

#####

PARTY OF ONE

Now, I know that sounds like a lot. Quite honestly, it is. It's a lot of work, but it does not have to be dreadful. The good news is you can enjoy being single **AND** work on all of those things at the same time! You can sit down, write down goals in the areas you need improvement, and go to work on those things. If you're struggling to hear from God, spend more time reading your Bible and meditating. Attend Word-based church services and church functions. They will allow you to not only hear from God, but also to meet people and form wonderful friendships. Those friendships can very well be the thing God uses to perfect those things that concern you. Doing them means you realize the true benefit of preparation.

Here's a tip: Do not go places for the sole purpose of meeting a woman. Go to learn and enjoy. If you go with the mentality that you're going to have a good time, there will be less pressure on you. Hence, if you don't meet anyone to your liking, you will not leave disappointed.

I have male friends whom I love dearly. Some are married. Some are single. When we get together, we talk about everything from current events to sports to pop culture. We eat together. We pray for one another. There has never been a time I have not wanted to get together with them just because there's no potential for a relationship. It is never a waste of my time to spend time with them. As a matter of fact, for the last few years, I have looked forward to getting together with them to watch the Super Bowl! We eat good food (thanks to my friend's wife), talk, laugh, and enjoy the game. When we have to part and go our separate ways at the end of the evening, the only sadness I feel is from having to separate from them until the next time. I always go home energized and looking forward to the next get-together, whether it be in one month or one year.

YOU WERE BORN TO LEAD

I encourage you to enjoy your life with your family, male friends, *AND* female friends. Go on vacations. Take a class. Hook up with your boys in somebody's "man cave", watch games, and talk. The time you spend enjoying your life is the best investment you can make because it represents your time. Time is something you either use wisely or waste. Trust me; if you waste too much of your time complaining and pouting about your loneliness, you will face a lot of regret. The more time you focus on preparing for your wife while enjoying life, the less time you have to complain about loneliness.

One last word to the men: If you don't remember anything else, please remember this:

A WOMAN WILL NOT FILL THAT EMPTY HOLE IN YOUR SOUL!

If you feel incomplete and lonely, you are wrong to think it's because you need a woman. The emptiness in you is where a special relationship with God belongs. No one else can fill that void, regardless of how much they love you or how hard they try to please you. No person is your all-in-all. Many men have gone through numerous women because they are looking for that special person to close that huge hole in their soul. It will never happen. Put God first, develop an intimate and personal love relationship with Him, and you'll see how much better your other relationships will develop. That's God's promise.

PARTY OF ONE

Questions (for Men) to Ponder from Chapter 6

1. Why do you think everything was already prepared for Eve before she was created?

YOU WERE BORN TO LEAD

2. Take a minute to meditate on your spiritual life. What are some things you can do to assure you that you are hearing the voice of God?

_____

_____

_____

_____

_____

_____

_____

_____

_____

_____

_____

_____

_____

_____

3. Why do you think it is so important for man to know his purpose prior to seeking a serious relationship?

_____

_____

_____

_____

_____

_____

_____

_____

_____

_____

_____

_____

_____

_____

_____

_____

_____

4. Think about your past hurts and failed relationships. Have you healed from all your emotional baggage? If not, how are you going to ensure your healing from past wounds?

_____
_____
_____
_____
_____
_____
_____
_____
_____
_____
_____
_____
_____
_____

PARTY OF ONE

5. Four important words: **How are your finances?**

Chapter 7

Submission and the Single Christian

Submit (verb): *To give over or yield to the power or authority of another; to come under.*

Let me start this chapter by asking a question. In your own words, what is your understanding of the word 'submission'?

_____

_____

_____

_____

'Submission' is one word that has been misused and abused not only in the world, but also in the church. The first thing I want to make clear is this: Submission is for **everyone**.

> *"But I would have you know, that the head of every man is Christ, and the head of the woman is the man; and the head of Christ is God."*
> (1 Corinthians 11:3)

> *"Yea, all of you be subject one to another, and be clothed with humility; for God resisteth the proud and give grace to the humble."*
> (1 Peter 5:5)

PARTY OF ONE

Just the mention of the word 'submission' makes some people cringe. It used to have the same effect on me. Honestly, the only time I heard the word used was in church - and most days, it was used incorrectly! Over time, I've learned that people don't respond well to being made to feel like they don't have a say in the decisions that affect their lives. The way the word was ministered to me in the past gave me the impression it was something used on married women so their husbands could control them. The very mention of the word stirred up anger in me.

As much as I wanted to be married, I was determined I would never submit to my husband. I decided we would be co-partners, and I would have the right to make just as many decisions concerning our family as he would have.

After studying the Bible more closely, I began to understand that submission is not a bad word. Actually, submission equals protection. When you think about family relationships, we find a perfect example of how Jesus and God relate to each other - and how they relate to us. When you think about family, Jesus is submitted to God and, therefore, protected by God. Jesus is the head of man. Man is submitted to Jesus and, therefore, protected by God **AND** Jesus. From this, we see that the husband is the head of the wife. The wife is submitted to her husband and, therefore, protected by God, Jesus, *AND* her husband.

You might be thinking, *"I'm single. What does submission have to do with me?"* The answer is **EVERYTHING**. Remember: Ephesians 5:21 says to submit yourselves to one another. You may desire a mate, but you are not prepared for a mate until you learn to submit. You can start practicing submission now by submitting to your Pastor and your Manager/Supervisor at work - just to name a couple. If you are a man with a woman supervisor, doing so will be great practice for you especially.

SUBMISSION AND THE SINGLE CHRISTIAN

You may not agree with all the ways your manager chooses to manage, but you are obligated to submit - whether you agree or not. You may even be in a position to express your concerns, but because that manager has been placed in authority over you, his or her word is the final authority. As long as that person is not asking you to do anything immoral or illegal, you are obligated to submit to that authority.

Let's say your manager asks you to do something you are confident will yield negative results. You express your concerns and he or she still insists on doing it his or her way. Because you are submitted to their authority, you carry out their orders and lo and behold: The results are negative. Guess what? You are protected because you carried out the instructions of the one who, as your manager, is in authority and responsible for the results! It is that person - not you - who must give an account to those in authority over him or her. If your company has integrity, you will not be blamed for your submission. There is protection in submission.

Men, when you become a husband, remember God is in authority over you. You must give an account for what you do. Each has to give an account to God for both submission and leadership. If you think a submitted person is a weak person, you are 100% wrong. Jesus is submitted to His Father, and there is absolutely **NOTHING** weak about Jesus!

As a child, I remember growing up having to submit to my mother's rules for her home. As a teenager, I despised rules. I must have said to myself a thousand times, "*I will be so glad when I grow up and get out of her house so nobody can tell me what to do!*" Well, I'm all grown up, on my own, and am still submitting to the authority of others - except now, because I understand submission, it's not dreadful.

PARTY OF ONE

Think about it: We have to submit to those over us at work, at church, etc. Even if we spend a few days at someone else's house, we have to follow their rules. If we're in the library and the librarian says, **"Shhhh!"**, we are obligated to be quiet. We submit in the grocery store when the sign says, "No Shoes. No shirt. No service." If we step foot into a courtroom, we all submit to the judge. If we're pulled over by the police, we submit to their authority.

I have learned that in this life, whether you want to submit or not, **YOU WILL**. Therefore, men, because you understand what submission is (and you *WILL* have to submit to others), you will come to appreciate your wife's submission to you. Likewise, women who have others submit to them will understand the responsibility your husband has being responsible for the well-being of others who are submitted to him.

I have to admit: Men bear a lot of responsibility in the family. God has given them a lot of responsibility, including protecting and providing for their family. It would be very stressful to be a man with a lot of responsibility over a family, yet married to a woman who doesn't respect him enough to submit to him. Men must be led by God, and if you trust a man enough to marry him, then you should feel confident in his leadership, and therefore submit to his God-given authority.

On the flipside of that, men also need to have enough wisdom to know when God has given certain gifts to their wives and allow her to operate in her gifts without being jealous or insecure. If a woman is better at managing the family's finances, then you (man) should allow her to do that.

Part of being a great leader is recognizing gifts in others and knowing how to delegate!

SUBMISSION AND THE SINGLE CHRISTIAN

If you're reading this book, you are most likely single. You can start practicing submission at work, at church, etc. You will know you are growing in this area when you can submit to those in authority without murmuring and complaining.

PARTY OF ONE

Questions to Ponder from Chapter 7

1. Has your understanding of submission changed after reading this chapter?

SUBMISSION AND THE SINGLE CHRISTIAN

2. Think about your daily life. Who are some of the people you can begin submitting to?

PARTY OF ONE

3. Think about the life of Christ. In what ways did He express submission to His Heavenly Father?

SUBMISSION AND THE SINGLE CHRISTIAN

4. Keeping Jesus in mind, how did He express submission to his earthly parents?

PARTY OF ONE

5. How do you treat those who are submitted to you?

Chapter 8

But God, Sex is Good!
Sex and the Single Christian

"Know ye not that ye are the temple of God, and that the Spirit of God dwelleth in you?"
(1 Corinthians 3:16)

Empty (adjective): *Containing nothing; having none of the usual or appropriate contents. Vacant; unoccupied.*

It's almost impossible to have an adult discussion about being single without tackling the subject of sex. This is the hardest chapter in this book for me to write. Why? Because to tackle this subject means being somewhat vulnerable.

First, let me explain why I began this chapter by defining the word 'empty'. That is exactly the feeling most singles expressed to me about how they feel after having sex with someone they are not married to. Sometimes, the empty feeling comes immediately after the act. Other times, it's hours or even days later. Rest assured, however; the feeling of emptiness does come.

I wish I could write this chapter out of a place of success. I wish I could tell you that I've practiced abstinence since becoming a Christian. However, I can't tell that lie. What I can do is convey some of the mistakes I've made in hopes that you don't repeat those same mistakes.

PARTY OF ONE

The Purpose of Sex

If you want to know the purpose of a thing, you must go to the creator of that thing to find out why he or she created it. So, it makes sense that we go to the Creator of sex - **GOD** - to find out why He created it.

In my reading of God's Word, I found three reasons God created sex. You might find more. Let's take a look at each one.

1. Procreation

> *"And God blessed them; and God said to them, **'Be fruitful and multiply, and fill the Earth**, and subdue it; and rule over the fish of the sea and over the birds of the sky, and over every living thing that moves on the Earth'."*
> (Genesis 1:28)

In Genesis 1:28, God was speaking to Adam and Eve. At the time God was speaking to them, He was also speaking to you and me. In order to continuously fill the Earth, we have to get married and have babies. Now, we all know how babies are created. If we all were to follow God's laws, our lives would look something like this:

Man meets woman.
Man and woman fall in love.
Man and woman marry.
Man and wife create children…
And the cycle continues.

Sexual intercourse is how we keep life on Earth multiplying.

BUT GOD, SEX IS GOOD!

Man + Woman + Sex = Procreation (Children)

"And Adam knew Eve his wife; and she conceived, and bare Cain, and said, 'I have gotten a man from the LORD'."
(Genesis 4:1)

2. Physical Pleasure

"May he kiss me with the kisses of his mouth. For your love is better than wine."
(Song of Solomon 1:2)

God promised us that He would withhold no good thing from those of us who walk uprightly. God created sex to be good, so why would He want to withhold it from us? He doesn't. But because of sin, sex has become selfish, self-serving, and self-centered. This creates broken hearts, broken homes, and broken values. Sex in marriage is as much about our protection as it is about intimacy. He wants us to enjoy the physical pleasure of sex, but He wants it done His way: within the sanctity of marriage.

God is your Father and His heart is turned towards protecting you. One reason He doesn't want you partaking of this physical pleasure with just anyone is because He cares about you - spirit, soul, and body. God knows that when two are joined together intimately, their souls are bound together and they become one flesh. Some people refer to this as a "soul-tie".

PARTY OF ONE

Have you or someone you know ever been intimately involved with someone and five years after the breakup, they still feel tied to that person? That's because when they came together and had sex, their souls became one. More likely, after the relationship fell apart, one or both persons ended up hurt or distraught. That is the very thing God is trying to protect you from. He knows you are likely going to date several people before you settle on one to marry, and He doesn't want your soul tied to every person you've ever dated.

There are some basic necessities in life: air, water, food, etc. There is a good chance if you don't get these things, you will die. Note that sex is not one of those things listed as a basic necessity. You might think you will die from lack of sex, but trust me; you are not going to die. You can wait. **WE** can wait.

3. **Intimacy**

   "Your two breasts are like two fawns, twins of a gazelle, which feed among the lilies."
   (Song of Solomon 4:5)

   "Let his left hand be under my head and his right hand embrace me."
   (Song of Solomon 2:6)

Being intimate includes sex - but it is not exclusively sex. Intimacy is the act of allowing someone to see who we really are and they, in turn, allow us to see who they really are.

BUT GOD, SEX IS GOOD!

Dr. Myles Munroe often preached on the topic of purpose. He often stressed that if you don't know the purpose of a thing, you will abuse it. We all need to be reminded of the purpose of sex because it is so easy to abuse it. God never intended for us to abuse the gift of sex by engaging in it outside the sanctity of marriage.

Protected versus Unprotected Sex

If you're thinking that you're okay as long as you use contraceptives for protection, then you are 100% wrong. Can I tell you something? **Outside of marriage, there is no such thing as 'protected sex'.**

All of my Christian life, I have always felt the safest when I am sure I am in the center of God's will. There has never been a time in my life when I was doing everything right, but there have been more times than not when I was at least conscience of my decisions and trying to do what was right. For me, being in the center of God's will is like walking in the rain with an umbrella. There is rain all around me, but it is not touching me because I'm protected by the covering of the umbrella. Stepping from under the umbrella puts me in a place where I will surely get wet. It is the same with being obedient to God. When we step from under His umbrella of protection by being disobedient, we are opening ourselves up to all kinds of attacks. Part of living a successful single life is choosing to abstain from sex until you are married. Choosing to do otherwise makes us vulnerable to the enemy (Satan).

I already know what questions are running through your mind while you're reading this. They are questions I've asked myself (and God) numerous times.

"What if I never get married? Do I have to live the rest of my life in abstinence?"

PARTY OF ONE

Good questions! Since whatever I say might not be well-received, I'll let the Apostle Paul do all the talking:

"Now for the matters you wrote about: "It is good for a man not to have sexual relations with a woman." But since sexual immorality is occurring, each man should have sexual relations with his own wife, and each woman with her own husband."
(1 Corinthians 7:1-2)

I have searched from Genesis to Revelation, and I am here to tell you: There is **no** loophole out of abstaining from sex outside of marriage. If you have a heart after God and want to please Him, you will have to abstain. Paul said it is better to marry than to burn with passion. Don't mistake Paul's statement by thinking it's okay to enter into an unholy marriage just so you don't burn with passion. Sex is a benefit of marriage, but it's certainly not the only or even primary reason to marry.

If you are struggling with sexual immorality, don't feel condemned. There is a way out. You are not the only one who is/was in that situation. I am a perfect example of how you can be delivered from the snares of the enemy when it comes to sexual sin.

Following are two examples from the Bible that outline sexual sins and the consequences of those sins:

BUT GOD, SEX IS GOOD!

David and Bathsheba (2 Samuel 11:1-12:23)	Reuben and Bilhah (Genesis 35:22; Genesis 48:1)
David slept with Uriah's wife, Bathsheba. Bathsheba became pregnant with David's child.	Reuben, Israel's first-born son, slept with his (Israel's) concubine, Bilhah.
David calls Uriah home from battle to get him to sleep with his wife in an attempt to cover his (David's) sin. *When that didn't work...*	Israel heard of Reuben's betrayal but didn't immediately confront him.
David had Uriah killed in battle.	*Genesis 48:1* Israel became sick. *Genesis 49:1-2* Israel began to pray blessings over his children and grandchildren.
God sends the prophet Nathan to rebuke David.	*Genesis 49:3-4* Israel reveals to Reuben that he is aware that he slept with his concubine. He referred to Reuben as unstable as water and informed him that he shall not excel.
David repents. Nathan warns David of the consequences of his sin: His child with Bathsheba will die.	As a result of his sin, Reuben did not receive the blessing of the first-born from his father, Israel.
The child becomes ill and dies.	

PARTY OF ONE

As you can see from the chart, there are external consequences to sexual sin. There are also internal consequences, which can include self-esteem issues. So, how do we - as singles - protect ourselves from the snares of sexual immorality? Good question! Following are a few suggestions:

1. **If your sexual desires are becoming a problem for you, then you should guard your eyes, ears, and mouth.**

    In other words, be careful what you watch, listen to, and say. If you are in the habit of watching pornography, stop now. Even certain movies and television shows can stir up images and thoughts. You should take a break from watching movies and TV shows with a lot of sexual content. Some music artists are known for sensual lyrics in their music.

    When this became a problem for me, I made it a point to only listen to gospel music. I traded in Barry White, Luther Vandross, and Marvin Gaye for Yolanda Adams, Donnie McClurkin, and Kirk Franklin. Music is very powerful. It actually triggers the release of dopamine - the pleasure chemical which the brain produces when we are stimulated in a pleasurable way. Dopamine is the same chemical that gets released when we eat our favorite food or buy something we want. If you notice, one of the most powerful things about music is the ability to remain in our thoughts all day. Have you ever heard a song on the radio and ended up singing it all day? You're spending your day speaking words over and over…and over.

BUT GOD, SEX IS GOOD!

I remember when Marvin Gay's song, "Sexual Healing", was in my head all day, even while at work. I found myself singing it quietly to myself throughout the entire day. No wonder I fell into sin. I kept repeating those words... *"When I get that feeling, I need sexual healing..."* until my words eventually became my reality.

2. **Be careful of flattery and flirtation.**

    Many affairs start out with what is perceived as "innocent" flattery and flirtation. It usually seems innocent at the beginning, but in the end, it leads to a place of no return. If you are already lonely and unhappy about your single status, you can definitely get caught up in this snare.

    Just for a man to have a woman notice how great he looks or a man notice a woman's new hair color and, in turn, compliment her on it can lead down a slippery slope. That's not to say every time someone compliments you, it's flirtation. **BUT** you do have to be careful if that same person is constantly bombarding you with compliments on a daily basis.

3. **Dress modestly.**

    Dressing immodestly is another snare that can get you caught up. A wise woman once said to a group of women, *"Be careful how you dress because if you're willing to show it, some men think you're willing to give it away."* Men and women should be careful not to dress in ways that are too provocative as to draw the wrong type of man/woman to you. If you dress in lustful fashion, you will draw lustful people to you.

4. Stop accepting fornication as 'just a part of life'.

Too many of us (myself included) have excused our behavior by saying, "*I'm human. I have needs*". We're all human! The Maker of humanity created us with those desires, but they have become tainted by sin. With faith and God's help, we can live the true life God has for us within the boundaries that we are all expected to respect and obey. These boundaries are set to protect us from the snares of the enemy.

5. Have an accountability partner.

If abstinence is a struggle for you, ask someone you trust to become your accountability partner. Ask them to hold you accountable for your decisions. Be willing to be open and honest about where you are and ask them to help you make good decisions by reminding you to not put yourself in compromising situations. Stay within the boundaries you (and your accountability partner) have set up for you.

6. Recognize when you are vulnerable.

We all know there are times when we are strong and times when we are weak. If you are in a place in your life where you feel weak and feel that you might not be able to abstain from sexual sin, that is the time you should opt out of dates - or choose to instead, date in groups only. And for goodness sake: Don't invite someone of the opposite sex to your home for a candlelight dinner with music playing and the lights down low! Doing that will create an atmosphere that makes it almost impossible to escape temptation.

BUT GOD, SEX IS GOOD!

As you continue your walk as a single person, I encourage you to seek God and surround yourself with people who are on the same path of sexual purity. If you find yourself in a relationship with someone who struggles to respect your decision to remain celibate until marriage, that is a good sign you are possibly dating the wrong person. Seek God for guidance and, if He leads you to end the relationship, do so...immediately.

PARTY OF ONE

Questions to Ponder from Chapter 8

1. Are there things you need to eliminate (even if only temporary) from your life to ensure you live a life that is sexually-pure (i.e., TV shows, movies, music, websites, etc.)?

BUT GOD, SEX IS GOOD!

2. Do you agree with my statement, "*Outside of marriage, there is no protected sex*"? Why or why not?

PARTY OF ONE

3. Do you think David's punishment (the death of his child) was justifiable for his sexual sins?

BUT GOD, SEX IS GOOD!

4. Thinking about the story of Israel, Reuben, and Bilhah, why do you think Israel waited so long to confront his son about sleeping with his concubine?

PARTY OF ONE

5. Do you believe a lifestyle of abstinence is reasonable for adult singles?

Chapter 9

Being Single is NOT a Curse

Curse: *To call or bring down evil on; an evil that has been invoked upon one.*

Once I made the transition to desiring marriage versus being desperate for marriage, I began to really enjoy my single life. I began to realize how blessed I am to be able to commit to the things of God without having to balance that against the responsibilities of marriage. I spent about 13 years of my life ministering to men and women in jails and prisons. It was a joy! There were times when I was at one county jail so much, you would have thought I was employed there. At one point, I went to the county jail on Mondays to teach a life skills class. On Wednesdays, I was at a different facility teaching the same type of class. On Fridays, I was at another for Friday night Bible Study. Once a month on Sunday afternoons, was my Bible study class at the jail. When I wasn't at work or at the jail, I was studying and preparing to go to the jail.

Prison Ministry was a very important part of my life, and I invested an exorbitant amount of my personal time in it. I had a full-time job, but my mind was always on the ladies and men I was called to minister to. I was always thinking of ways to make their lives behind bars more tolerable.

Since my son was an adult by that time, I stopped cooking on a regular basis. At one point, I would either skip dinner or eat out (not recommended). The times I ate out at a restaurant, I would carry my ministry materials with me to read, dreaming up ways to teach a lesson that would be relevant to inmates.

PARTY OF ONE

When I did eat at home, Honey Nut Cheerios with bananas and almond milk became my favorite meal. With the responsibilities of marriage and family, would I have had time for all of that? No. Although I had a desire to be married, I was happy and content as a single.

Now, you tell me what husband would have put up with that for any extended period of time? Not many. But I was happy and very content. After I had a change of heart about being single, I began to enjoy the ministry even more. That was one of the best seasons of my life! Instead of focusing on what I didn't have (a husband), I rerouted all of that energy to serving God by serving others. Was I a little off-balance? Yep! *BUT* I was the happiest and most-fulfilled off-balance woman on planet Earth.

My point is this: You are not cursed because you are not married. Never look at being single as something you're just tolerating until that special person comes along. Think of being single as a blessing - whether that blessing is temporary or permanent. I will gladly share with you some of the benefits I enjoy as a single person. I hope as you read them, you will realize you are enriched with the same benefits. You need to see them as a blessing…instead of a curse.

Come. Walk with me…

BEING SINGLE IS NOT A CURSE

1. I have become a lot more disciplined.

I know if something needs to be done - especially around my house - I better get up and get it done. I don't have the luxury of having another person to depend on to get it done. So, if it's going to get done, I'll be the one doing it! Since I am not skilled to do everything, I have to sometimes spend money hiring someone to do it for me. However, those things I can do myself, I do them.

I remember once, my garage door would not go all the way down when I used my remote control. That meant every time I needed to go somewhere, I had to back the car out of the garage, get out of the car, walk back into the garage, and let the door down with the wall button. After letting the door down, I had to exit out of the living room door, lock the front door, get in the car, and **THEN** go. Now, you know that grew old *VERY* quickly. After about three weeks of doing that, one day out of the blue, I had this bright idea! I went on YouTube and searched "garage door will not go all the way down" and, of course, YouTube did not disappoint. I watched the video as the instructor gave step-by-step instructions on how to get that door working again. I followed his instructions, and two minutes later, the door was fully operational.

PARTY OF ONE

Now, you're probably saying, "*But if you were married, you wouldn't have to worry about that.*" Well, I sure hope that's true, but guess what? I'm not married. I had a problem that needed a solution. I can't sit around and wait for my knight in shining armor to come along and fix my problem. For me, the best part is that I took the initiative to learn something I didn't know. To me, learning new things is priceless because it gives me a sense of accomplishment, regardless if it's something huge or something small.

2. **I've overcome loneliness.**

I've always loved going to the movies, but if I wasn't in a relationship, I would always call a friend to go with me. If a friend wasn't available, there were times I didn't go until that friend became available. No more of that. When there's a movie I want to see, 95% of the time, I go see the movie alone. After the movie, there have been times I take myself out to dinner. After that, I'm back home either reading a good book or chatting with friends on the phone. This might seem small to some, but that is how I learned to love spending time alone with the person I love… **ME!**

For the past few years, it has been nothing for me to put on nice clothes, make-up, comb my hair, and take myself out for an elegant dinner. I enjoy it. That has helped me to really get to know myself better and become more observant of the world around me. Let me tell you some things I've observed when I'm alone at a table enjoying my dinner.

BEING SINGLE IS NOT A CURSE

I've seen couples come in the restaurant, sit at the table, and never have a conversation. When I'm having dinner alone, it makes sense that I'm not having a conversation with anyone, but a couple not talking to each other? That's ludicrous! I once observed a couple that literally talked more to their waitress than they did to each other. I once remember thinking to myself, "*I would rather spend the rest of my life single than to be in a relationship with someone with whom we have absolutely nothing to talk about.*" Now **THAT'S** what I call lonely!

I'll never forget one January day one of my close friends treated me to dinner for my birthday at Mary Mac's Tea Room in Atlanta. As she and I were sitting there enjoying our dinner and catching up on what was going on in our lives, a middle-aged couple was escorted to a table near us. My friend (who pays attention to **everything** around her) observed that after sitting at the table for at least 20 minutes, the couple hadn't said one word to each other since they sat down. The man was actually on his iPhone reading his Facebook page, while his woman sat there looking bored out of her mind. I remember telling my friend how it would have been better for the lady to have dinner alone because essentially, that's what she was doing anyway.

PARTY OF ONE

3. I can do what I want, for as long as I want, whenever I want. In other words, I have a lot of personal freedom.

My church has two Sunday morning services. Sometimes I attend the first service; other times, the second. There's no rhyme or reason behind my decision to go early or late. I make that decision Sunday morning when I get up, and it's usually made based simply on how I feel at the moment.

Most days when I get off work, I change clothes and work out. For dinner, I'll probably pick up something microwaveable since it'll be too late to cook. Then, I'll either spend time reading or watching something on TV, after which I go to bed. I love my personal freedom. I'm sure if I were married, whether to go to church early or late, how much time I spend alone at the library, or how late I work would be things I would have to think twice about. After all, my decisions would affect someone other than myself.

Another example of personal freedom: I once spent a week trying to decide if I should trade in my car that I purchased two years prior in order to upgrade to a newer model. I did not have to check with anyone before making said decision. It was a decision I made by just asking God and weighing my options. Without the responsibility of marriage, I was able to make the decision myself without considering how it would affect others in the household.

BEING SINGLE IS NOT A CURSE

I plan to begin the process of selling my home and buying another one. I now have a desire to live somewhere that is more pedestrian-friendly with sidewalks and bicycle trails. I also want the neighborhood to have more grocery stores and restaurants within walking distance of my house. Oh, and yes: I want to live in the city. Yep! I don't mind hearing the sounds of traffic, sirens, and children playing *(as long as they're in the house by the time the street lights come on)*. At this age, I imagine if I were married, he'd be ready to settle down in the suburbs where it's quiet and where fewer people reside.

Well, I'm single, so I get to have the desires of my heart without having to consider another person's desire that could very well be totally opposite of mine. With the responsibilities of marriage, I would have to take into consideration the desires of others, which would need to be negotiated with some compromise. That is not a bad thing, but while I have the freedom to do certain things, it's okay to do them!

4. **I have learned what it means to wholly trust and rely on God.**

Now, this is one benefit I wouldn't trade - even for Mark Zuckerberg's money! There have been times when money was scarce or I was in excruciating physical pain or someone tried to break into my house. I had to trust *God* to take care of me.

When I think of all the things God has done for me, I think of a resume. A resume is a written document outlining your past work history, accomplishments, etc. Well, God's resume with me is *overwhelming*. The reason I can trust God now is because of His resume...His track record. I have testimony after testimony of the many wonderful times God has come through for and protected me when I was in harm's way. I am confident God will always show up on my behalf. This type of confidence only comes from experience. I can read about God's goodness and listen to sermons about God's goodness, but those things cannot compare to experiencing God's goodness for myself.

5. **I love myself more.**

The greatest commandment is to love God with all your heart, soul, and mind. The second greatest commandment is like unto the first, and that is to love your neighbor as you would yourself. Who is my 'neighbor'? **Everybody!** That tells me in order to love others, I must first know how to love myself. I learned to love myself more when I realized that regardless of what I do (or fail to do), God will always love me perfectly. I also learned to love myself more when I learned to accept myself just as I am while embracing my flaws. I no longer compare myself to others. I only compete with myself and I've learned to not complain about what I don't have. I am truly appreciative for what I do have. I no longer care if someone doesn't embrace me because of what I look like, or the color of my skin, or because I'm too short or too tall. I don't need validation by a man or anyone else. I have been validated by my Father.

BEING SINGLE IS NOT A CURSE

I feel great in the beautiful skin God put me in, and I wouldn't trade who I am for anything. I was born into a great family and was raised in a great city. I purposely surround myself with wonderful people who I love and who love me. This is me. I am who God intended me to be. I was born at the exact time, on the exact date, in the exact month, within the exact year that God ordained for me. I am uniquely me - just as you are uniquely you. I'm right where God wants me to be. I'm happy, healthy, and looking forward to the next phase of my life. I have a great life. I didn't say a perfect life, but it certainly qualifies as a great life!

God loves us with all of our flaws right now, even as He works to shape us into the people He is calling us to be. He loved me yesterday, He loves me now, and He will love me tomorrow. His love encourages me to let God have His way in my life, make whatever changes He needs to make as He makes me more Christ-like, and prepares me for the purpose He has for me.

Over the years, I have met a lot of men and women who saw being single as a curse and became desperate for marriage. I must say that the number of women far exceeds the number of men. I know exactly how they feel because I used to be one of them. If that's you, I want to encourage you to do the following…

PARTY OF ONE

Trust God

Seriously. I mean it. I know it sounds sort of "cliché-ish", but it's vital that you do just that. I was told to do that over a million times by everyone - from family to friends to clergy. In my heart of hearts, I honestly thought I was trusting God...but I wasn't. I realize now I didn't trust God at all. In fact, I walked in constant fear that God was not going to do what He promised He would do. Trust His timing, purpose, and goodness.

Don't become desperate.

Remember this: **"Desperate people do desperate things."** The easiest way to get into the wrong relationship is to become desperate.

During my years of waiting, I can now say with honesty: I became desperate. It still hurts to admit that and own up to my past desperation because it sounds so...let's see...**DESPERATE**! For me, desperation is embarrassing. Even though I created a list of "must-haves" for my future husband, I constantly ignored that list when I chose to date. As a Christian, I tried very hard to not date men who weren't Christians. Once or twice, I ignored my 'gut' and did it anyway.

BEING SINGLE IS NOT A CURSE

When you find yourself putting your desires before being obedient to God, **YOU'RE DESPERATE!** The sooner you recognize it, admit it, and quit it, the better off you will be. When you do that, your relationships (including those that are just friendships) should enhance you. If you are dating someone with whom you are not "equally yoked", you will not be enhanced. Relationships built while we are disobedient will not bring out the best in us. As a matter of fact, they will do just the opposite: bring you down. Being in a wrong relationship can affect every area of your life.

One of the things I noticed when I was in wrong relationships was that a spirit of depression would always come over me. Now, I'm not one who is prone to going into a state of depression, so I couldn't figure out why I would get out of bed feeling edgy, angry, and irritated. It was only after my eyes were opened that I equated my depression with my wrong relationship.

If you have unexplained bouts with depression, check your relationships. You might not need Xanax as much as you need to remove some people from your life…

PARTY OF ONE

Questions to Ponder from Chapter 9

1. Think about the definition of a 'curse'. Before you read this chapter, were you ever under the impression there was some type of curse attached to you that was preventing you from finding the love you desire?

_____
_____
_____
_____
_____
_____
_____
_____
_____
_____
_____
_____
_____
_____

BEING SINGLE IS NOT A CURSE

2. What are some things you can start doing **TODAY** to begin enjoying your single life?

PARTY OF ONE

3. Take an honest look at your life; your habits, your finances, your attitude, etc. Now, look at yourself in the mirror and ask yourself this one question: If you were the opposite sex, would you marry you? If the answer is no, why not? After you answer those two questions, make a list of things you need to change and write out a detailed plan on how you will change them. Then, work your plan!

BEING SINGLE IS NOT A CURSE

4. This chapter has been about appreciating your single life. List two things about being single that you truly enjoy and know you will miss if you were to get married.

_____
_____
_____
_____
_____
_____
_____
_____
_____
_____
_____
_____
_____
_____

PARTY OF ONE

5. Meditate on and write down two things that have you in bondage to your past. How will you overcome the guilt of your mistakes?

_____

_____

_____

_____

_____

_____

_____

_____

_____

_____

_____

_____

_____

_____

Chapter 10

Graced to Be Single
What if I Never Get Married?

In the short time I have been ministering to single people, the one question I am often asked is, *"What if I never get married?"* The question never surprises me. It's a question I have asked God numerous times myself, and it's a legitimate question. The truth is this: Some of us will never marry.

My answer to that question is: If God means for you to marry, you will marry. If He doesn't mean for you to marry, that means He has graced you to be single; you just need to accept it.

I know that's hard to accept, but I believe in my heart that it's the truth. Your enemy, Satan, would like nothing more than to have you live your single years in misery, feeling sorry for yourself, and being pitiful.

The first thing we all have to realize is that we were created to serve, love, and glorify God. God has a purpose for each of our lives, and if marriage doesn't fit into that purpose, then God will help you live out your years happily, joyfully…and single.

PARTY OF ONE

During a workshop I taught about being single and happy, I met a lady who was a widow. She and her husband had been married over 35 years before he passed away. I was so impressed with her because not only was she outwardly beautiful, she was also inwardly beautiful. She spoke about how she and her husband took care of each other while he was alive, how they raised their children, and enjoyed each other's company. Now that he was gone, she was living her life as a single, widowed woman - and she was at peace. That woman had no desire to remarry, but rather was seeking her next assignment from God. She wanted to travel with her friends, and enjoy her children, grandchildren, ministry, etc. Now, I'm not saying that every widow should desire to not remarry. I am, however, saying we should all learn to be content in whatever state we are currently living in. Remember that Paul said:

"I know how to live on almost nothing or with everything. I have learned the secret of living in every situation, whether it is with a full stomach or empty, with plenty or little. For I can do everything through Christ, who gives me strength."
(Philippians 4:12-13, NLT)

Now, the times that Paul was hungry and in lack were not enjoyable times. No one in their right mind enjoys being hungry or lacking the most basic of needs. However, Paul was stating that during the time when he was hungry and during the time when he had nothing, he learned to be content (satisfied with what one is or has). In other words, he learned to make the best of it.

Please learn from my experience: It does not profit you anything to complain about your situation.

Paul was hungry. Paul was in lack. Paul was imprisoned.

GRACED TO BE SINGLE

You are single. You are blessed. You are graced. You are favored. And you are all of those things and more with *OR* without a mate!

I have a question for you: What were you put on this Earth to accomplish? You know…your purpose? Everyone and everything that was created by God was created for a purpose - especially mankind. If you don't know your purpose, I suggest you spend some time fasting and praying so that God can reveal it to you. Once He reveals it (and He will), then it would be wise of you to get busy fulfilling that purpose. I believe if we would pursue our God-given purpose the way we pursue relationships, we would find ourselves living a phenomenal life.

I used to look back on the years I spent worrying about finding a mate and wondered what I could have accomplished during those times that I spent doing virtually nothing but complaining. How many people could have been ministered to if I hadn't been feeling sorry for myself and hosting my own pity parties? How much money could I have made if I had focused on building an empire instead of finding a husband? How many degrees could I have attained if I had only been focused on my purpose? I have since stopped looking back and thinking about 'woulda-shoulda-coulda'. I have moved on with my life, living it with purpose and enjoying each and every single day. I can't change the past, so I decided to move forward. I no longer live my life looking in the rearview mirror. I live my life looking ahead.

And so it is for you. Don't look back. Start from today and make a commitment to appreciate what you have. Celebrate the people in your life, pursue your purpose, and live your life to the fullest!

PARTY OF ONE

Questions to Ponder from Chapter 10

1. Have you ever asked God why you are not married? If so, have you received an answer? What is your response to His answer?

_____

_____

_____

_____

_____

_____

_____

_____

_____

_____

_____

_____

GRACED TO BE SINGLE

2. If you have never asked God why you are not married, is it because you are content being single **OR** is it because you are afraid of what His answer will be?

PARTY OF ONE

3. Do you know your purpose for being on this Earth? If so, are you operating in your purpose? If not, what are you waiting for? If you don't know your purpose, what steps are you going to take to figure out that purpose so you can pursue it?

_____

_____

_____

_____

_____

_____

_____

_____

_____

_____

_____

_____

4. Like Paul, have you ever had to learn to live in lack? If so, how did you handle it? Were you continuously stressed? What changed first: your attitude or your situation?

PARTY OF ONE

5. What if you never get married? Can you still live a happy, fulfilled life? **(Be honest.)**

Chapter 11

What to do While You Wait

One of the reasons single men and women find being single so difficult is because they are not actually "living" their lives. Life is fun! Let me say that again. **LIFE. IS. FUN!** Whether you live in the big city or a small farm town, life is fun! We all face challenges in life, but our life's challenges shouldn't keep us from enjoying our lives.

I discussed earlier about singles making the mistake of not taking their dream vacation 'until they find a suitable mate'. If you've been dreaming of going to Hawaii, Paris, Italy, or anywhere else, **GO**! Do not spend your life waiting on another person to join you before you can enjoy **LIFE**. I used to do that, and let me tell you; that's a very depressing way to live.

All of my adult life, I wanted to take a cruise. I didn't care about the cruise's destination: I just wanted to board a ship, lay out on the deck, eat, rest, and have a good time. I used to go online often looking at cruise ships and say to myself, "Just wait until I get married! My honeymoon will be on a cruise ship!" I would hear co-workers and friends talk about how much they loved cruising, and I still wouldn't ask a friend to go on a cruise with me. In my mind, I believed I wouldn't be able to enjoy myself unless I was with that 'special person'.

PARTY OF ONE

After I woke up out of my "waiting coma", I decided I would make my dream of taking a cruise a reality. So, I threw out the idea of a cruise to all four of my sisters. Two of them actually took the bait. One year later, we were boarding a Carnival cruise ship out of New Orleans headed to Cozumel, Mexico. After a fantastic night out enjoying New Orleans, the next morning we excitedly boarded the cruise ship for our four-day cruise. It was delightful! I did all the things I'd dreamed about. And you know what? I did take that cruise with 'someone special'! My sisters are special to me! They always have been and always will be.

Besides going on vacation, there are so many things you can do while you wait...

Go back to school.

If you've always wanted to get a degree (or another degree), this is a great time to do it. Unless you have minor children, you don't have to rush home to cook for anyone. Forget the laundry; you can get that done at midnight. You don't have anyone competing for your time. Even if you have a demanding job or career, you can make the time to study and attend classes. It'll be good to get out of the house a couple of nights a week and be around people who have like-interests.

When I decided to live my life to the fullest, I returned to school. I was so busy studying, writing papers, and reading, I didn't have time to get lonely or bored. As a matter of fact, I didn't really have time to sleep, much less anything else! With a full-time job and school, I had to learn to be a good steward of my time. Rarely did I go to bed before midnight - and when I climbed into bed, I was so tired, I didn't have time to think about anything but sleep.

WHAT TO DO WHILE YOU WAIT

Serve on a mission trip.

There are so many churches that sponsor mission trips, some of which you do not have to be a member to travel and serve. Although I've thought about it many times, I've never been on a mission trip. I have attended a couple of interest meetings and viewed videos of fellow church members who traveled to different countries. The work they perform on a mission trip is phenomenal. The idea of serving other people day in and day out is very humbling. When you experience the work these awesome people perform, you have absolutely no time to think about what you don't have. You're too busy serving others!

Make a list of things you've always wanted to do and do them... one by one.

If bungee-jumping is your thing, **DO IT!** If sky-diving is your thing, **DO IT!** You don't have to be about to die to make a Bucket List. If you've always wanted to sell homes, go to Real Estate school, get your license, and **GO FOR IT!** Start a book club. Become a barber. Write a book. Create a blog. Become a Baker. A Cake Decorator. A Wedding Planner. A Hair Braider. An Inventor. Become a Runner. Or a Cyclist. A Clothing Designer. Whatever it is that you've been meditating on for years, now is the time to **DO IT!** The beginning phase of anything you do is always time-consuming. Working on something you've always dreamed about will not only bring you joy, it will give you purpose!

PARTY OF ONE

Work on becoming the right person.

I remember listening to a tape of a minister speaking to single people. His topic was something related to preparing yourself to receive a mate from God. The man asked a million-dollar question - one I will never forget. His question was: *"Would you marry you?"* In other words, put yourself in the place of the opposite sex.

Now, imagine you met the person you are right now. Would you be impressed with this person (you) enough to consider a serious relationship with them (you)?

He continued: *"Do you hang up your clothes after you take them off after work or do you just clutter your bed with clothes? Would you do that if you were married? Well, stop doing it...now!"*

Wow! I was so convicted because I had a very bad habit of coming home from work, changing clothes, and hanging my work clothes on my treadmill.

We all have flaws, but it is perfectly reasonable to work on self-improvement. That needs to be done without the fear of failing or the pressure of trying to be perfect in the presence of another.

Attitude adjustment.

Are you a woman or man who loves drama? If you are, now would be a good time to change that attitude. Who wants to live with someone who is never happy? Would you want to be tied up with someone who always finds something to argue about? Are you a man or woman who fights every battle - instead of choosing your battles wisely? If the people you live with now have to come home to you and your unpredictable mood, you have a lot of work to do.

WHAT TO DO WHILE YOU WAIT

First, find out why you're never happy. Then, start working on being healed. If it's pain from a past relationship or marriage, make a decision to forgive and move on so that you can be whole. If necessary, seek counseling. I bet the person who hurt you has moved on, which is probably why you're still so bitter. Bitterness is not sexy. As a matter of fact, it's an awful character flaw that, if you possess it, needs to be worked on starting **NOW**! Not tomorrow…**NOW**! Stop being a victim and start creating the life you want today.

I want you to humor me for one minute.

Suppose God came to you and told you that exactly one year from today, He would be introducing you to your spouse. After you stop shouting, dancing, and praising God, what would you do to prepare for that person to enter your life? Well, those are the things you should be doing **RIGHT NOW!** So, go ahead and start exercising. Go ahead and get those bills paid off. Go ahead and forgive your ex, your mother, your dad. Go ahead and develop that prayer life and spend quality time in devotion with God.

Some of us have a long list of things we need to work on, and **NOW** is the time to do it. Today, you're a 'Party of One', but next year, you could be a party of (at least) two. Enjoy the journey!

PARTY OF ONE

Questions to Ponder from Chapter 11

1. We discussed adjusting your attitude in this chapter. Do you need an attitude adjustment? Is there some negativity in your life that you need to deal with? If so, what are you going to do to turn your negative into a positive?

_____

_____

_____

_____

_____

_____

_____

_____

_____

_____

_____

_____

_____

WHAT TO DO WHILE YOU WAIT

2. Do you have a Bucket List? May I suggest you start working on that list today? Take your dream vacation. Go back to school. Join an interest group. List below two things you can begin doing today to start working on that Bucket List. If you don't already have a Bucket List, then list two things you would put on that list if you had one. Now, go do them!

_____

_____

_____

_____

_____

_____

_____

_____

_____

_____

_____

PARTY OF ONE

3. We discussed working on becoming the right person. What are some bad habits you can currently work on quitting? Now would be a great time to work on those things while they do not affect another person.

_____

_____

_____

_____

_____

_____

_____

_____

_____

_____

_____

_____

_____

_____

WHAT TO DO WHILE YOU WAIT

4. What types of things can you do now to decrease the drama in your life?

Conclusion

I realize that everything in this book does not relate to everyone. However, it is my sincere hope and prayer that something in this book has inspired you to rethink how you feel about being single and how you live your single life. After living my entire life as a single person, I am ecstatic to announce I am currently engaged and plan to marry this year (2017). It was only after I began to work the principles in this book (which God led me to write) that I began to even attract the right kind of man in my life.

It was only after truly putting God first in my life, becoming a content and happy single, and being comfortable with who I am, that I became ready for a healthy relationship. Before I met my fiancé, I had a conversation with God. We came to the conclusion that regardless of whether He blessed me with a mate or not, I would live my life to the fullest…to the overflow. When I met my fiancé, I was busy doing what God called me to do: teaching singles how to live a happy and full life. I was happily working on me, working a full-time job, ministering to singles, and in the early stages of planning to take a dream vacation. Now, that dream vacation will be my honeymoon!

We all have regrets in our lives. We all have things we wish we would have done better. That's normal. However, don't allow the devil to add another regret; living a dull, sad, and desperate life as a single.

God wants us to be happy, have fun, and enjoy life. I challenge you to make a decision today to be the happiest single person in the world!

ABOUT THE AUTHOR

Author Loraine Bedford is originally from Shreveport, Louisiana. She currently resides in Atlanta, Georgia and has lived there for over 30 years.

A former Children's Ministry Teacher and Prison Ministry Bible Teacher, Loraine now teaches a *Successful Single Living* class for the singles at her local church.

Contact Loraine for speaking engagements by emailing her at: LoraineBedford@yahoo.com

www.ingramcontent.com/pod-product-compliance
Lightning Source LLC
Chambersburg PA
CBHW071737080526
44588CB00013B/2069